Bernhard J. Schmidt

Practice compact:

Autism and Dog

Bernhard J. Schmidt

Practice compact:
Autism and Dog

© 2019 Bernhard J. Schmidt,

Oberwarmensteinach, Germany
All Rights reserved.
ISBN: 978-3750419469

translated from
Praxis kompakt: Autismus und Hund
© 2017 Bernhard J. Schmidt,
ISBN: 978-3746062556

Production and Publishing:
BoD – Books on Demand, Norderstedt, Germany

Bibliographic information of the German National Library:
The German National Library lists this publication
in the German National Bibliography; detailed bibliographic
Data are available online at http://dnb.dnb.de.

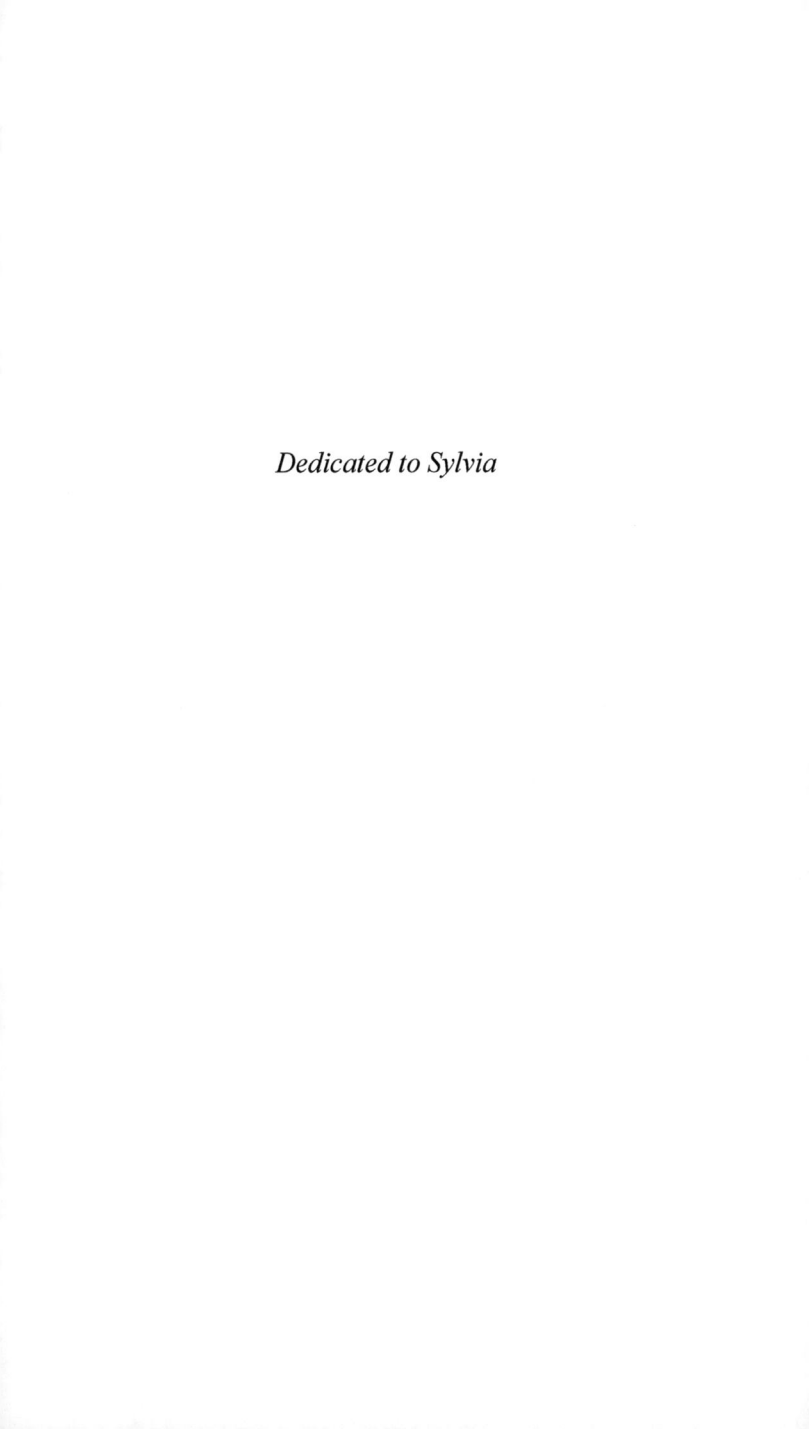

Dedicated to Sylvia

Table of content

I. PREFACE

While the books in the "Klartext kompakt" series primarily dealt with the theoretical background to the understanding of autism, this book deals above all with practical implementation.

The basis for this is the experience and conclusions derived from two areas:

1.) the Solidar Hotel Goldener Stern with the offer of holidays for families with (autistic) children, and

2.) Cooperation with the dog school Sylvia Ulrich, which we visit with our guests from the Solidar Hotel once a week.

The book is thus based on the experiences with the interaction of several autistic children, adolescents and adults aged 3 - 29 years with dogs.

And this under the perspective of the new social-psychological and developmental autism theory, which also shows anxiety and stress as the main problems in autistic people.

So reducing anxiety and stress is our main focus. Our experience at the Solidar Hotel shows very clearly how conducive this reduction in the whole family can be to the development of the autistic child.

In addition to a low-stimulus environment as well as

facilities of the hotel, it is above all the acceptance of, against neurotypic people, other behavior of autistic people.

The big advantage of the experience at the Solidar Hotel is that you not only experience the whole family, but also for a whole week. The relaxation offered does not only affect the autistic children, but also the whole family.

We were able to experience autistic children and adolescents, who hit their heads against the wall on the first day or stood in the stairwell facing the wall for a long time. And then with each day, together with the parents, more and more relaxed and opened more and more. A not insignificant part of these developments were the joint visits of all interested guests to the dog school of Sylvia Ulrich. Even though, at first sight, there was not much change in the one-hour visits to the dog school, we were able to see significant changes in the interaction within families in the following days.

In addition, there has been a special therapy dog in training at the Solidar Hotel for some time - our Krishna. This came after a career as a sled dog at the age of six and a half years in the hotel. The great advantage of Krishna is, in addition to his good-natured and tolerable nature, his willingness to cooperate and communicate with strangers. So he contributed from the beginning to

reduce stress and always conquers immediately the hearts of children in particular. The cover picture shows Marlene, 5 years old and mutist autistic, along with Krishna. Marlene's smile is worth a thousand words.
Both the visits to the dog school and the experiences with Krishna show us again and again how positively dogs can affect people in general and autistic people in particular. The book therefore deals extensively with the interaction between humans and dogs, as well as the question of how this can be made as profitable as possible. In order to keep the book as simple and understandable as possible, citations as well as theoretical discussions are omitted. Even though there are some studies on the fundamentally positive effects of dogs on the parents of autistic children as well as on themselves, this does not mean that the interaction between man and dog always works for both sides.
Therefore, the focus is mainly on the practical implementation of the interaction between humans and dogs.

My special thanks go to Sylvia Ulrich.
Without the experiences with their dogs in group lessons and without their advice, this book would not have been possible.

II. INTRODUCTION

To no other animal has man developed a closer
relationship than to the dog. For more than a thousand
years a very close symbiosis between man and dog has
developed. And no other animal can read the body
language and signals of humans better than the dog.
On the other hand, holding a dog is becoming more and
more fashionable at the moment. And unfortunately also
in a non-art and needs-appropriate attitude. Dogs are
developing diseases of civilization such as obesity and
mental disorders.
It has also developed a huge market, which suggests the
alleged satisfaction of alleged needs of dogs.
And also in the area of autism, dogs are now a big topic.
More and more families with autistic children hope that
the acquisition of a dog will improve the interaction and
promote the development of the autistic child.
The range of dogs purchased ranges from the rescued
street dog to a few thousand euros expensive assistance
dog.
Often, unfortunately, only the extremes of this large span
are perceived, ie either street dogs or expensive
assistance dogs.

13

The many possibilities in between are unfortunately too often overlooked.

And also in the selection of dog breed is often followed by fashion rather than reason. But not all dog breeds are equally suitable.

So it should not be surprising if it increasingly comes to problems in the coexistence of humans and dogs. And then the goal, namely the reduction of anxiety and stress and the promotion of social interaction, is missed. The dog is rarely the problem, but in many cases a misunderstanding of the needs of a dog and / or a non-species-appropriate attitude. First and foremost is the humanization of the dog, and thus a coddling.

The "right" dog in the right environment can act as a "catalyst", relieve stress, provide access to the autistic and enhance interaction. The "wrong" dog, on the other hand, does the opposite.

But "right" and "wrong" are not characteristics that the dog has in him, but that arise through the selection, attitude and guidance of the human being.

So the "right" dog does not just fall from the sky, but requires a level of competence that should not be underestimated. Competence in the selection of a suitable breed, the appropriate age and level of training of the dog, as well as the species-appropriate attitude and leadership.

And as helpful as dogs can be with autistic people and their families, they are never the answer.

So do not expect miracles from buying a dog.

III. AUTISM

The main difference between our understanding of autism and common belief is that autism is neither a disease nor a disability.

In our understanding, autism is another form of both perception and communication.

How comprehensive already explained in other books (see Bibliography at the end of the book), autistics have so far a different perception than the one often higher sensory sensitivity exists, on the other hand, above all, a "stimulus filters weakness" exists. This means that annoying stimuli are not automatically hidden.

However, we will focus here on the area of the particular form of communication and interaction of autistic individuals. For one thing, one goal of acquiring a dog is to improve social interaction with the autistic child. On the other hand, possible problems with the interaction with dogs as well as autistics are very similar in several respects. This is reflected again and again in the visits to the dog school, which we will discuss in more detail.

But how does autistic communication differ from neurotypical people?

NT people (neurotypical, not autistic) communicate to a

large extent unconsciously about facial expressions, gestures, modulation of the voice ...

This unconscious communication serves to guide the group, which works like a kind of "autopilot".

At the same time, group affiliation and position within the group structure are communicated via the unconscious group behavior.

However, unconscious group communication often causes NT people not to say what they mean; and do not mean what they say .

This (unconscious) side of communication thus serves the question of, and orientation on the group's opinion. It is embossed e.g. through small-talk and many (superfluous) words as a form of grooming.

Autists lack this side of communication in two ways. On the one hand they can not communicate in this way, on the other they do not understand this communication and therefore can not orientate themselves to the group.

So it lacks the "autopilot".

The lack of unconscious (group) communication and interaction can disrupt the social (!) Interaction. But social interaction is an essential basis for development - of man and dog. By disrupting social interaction, for example in autistics often by bullying and exclusion by groups, it can then result in a disruption of development. Our understanding of the importance of social interaction and communication, etc. as a basis for development, it also means that we are not only concerned with the autistic people, but with the whole family. Because communication and interaction is something that always takes place between corresponding communication partners. So if there is a disruption of social interaction, then all partners are involved, not just the autistic person. Therefore, we also consider the effect of dogs not only on autistic people, but also on the whole family. And as we shall see, it is often just the shift of attention away from the autistic human who can break new ground.

1   Autistics and Dogs

The aim of this section is not to put dogs with autism on a par. The differences between autistic and dog far outweigh the similarities. And yet it seems sensible to examine the existing similarities in more detail.
We do not want to humanize dogs, nor do we want to equate autistic behavior with dogs.
But arrogance towards other mammals is also not appropriate. For evolution has not invented new (survival) strategies for every species, but many are found in different species. And especially the social behavior of mammals, which includes both humans and dogs, is similar in many areas.

Although many books have been written about autism, autistics and even dogs, and these should not be repeated here.
But looking at the similarities between autistic people and dogs can be enlightening and helpful. And also to answer the question, why the interaction between man and dog is also and especially good for autistic people.

1.1   Sensory Abilities

Autists often have a much more pronounced sensory perception of the environment, so in comparison to NT people hypersensitivity. This means that autistic people often not only see, smell and hear better, but are also particularly sensitive to touch.
And dogs can smell and hear even better.
This difference in perception is often overlooked by caregivers as well as dog owners. People tend to think that their own perception is the measure of all things.
Many people find it hard to be aware of the effects of higher sensory sensitivity in autistic people and dogs and to get an idea of it. An irritated environment can cause stress in autistic people as well as animals due to the more sensitive perception. Stress as well as a physical reaction that influences among other things heartbeat, blood pressure and digestion. As well as in the form of an

accompanying "flight or fight" condition. This stress, as vital as it may be to some extent, does not only cause physical problems as a permanent condition, but above all it hinders social interaction!

1.2   Communication

For dogs, the "natural" environment has changed. If it was still with the ancestors, the wolves, the pack in a natural environment, then coexistence with humans takes place in a technical, artificial world.

If there are dogs in the pack, the communication and interaction still works, as with the wolves, according to the rules of the dogs. In contrast, communication between humans and dogs is much more difficult and it can easily lead to misunderstandings.

Although dogs have learned over millennia, especially to interpret the body language and facial expressions of people very successfully. However, this must not lead to the fallacy that dogs on the one hand understand the phonetic language of humans, nor that dogs are dependent on spoken language as "social grooming", ie on small-talk.

How pronounced the ability of mammals can be to understand man's facial expressions is impressively demonstrated by the example of "clever Hans".

1.2.a   Excursus: The clever Hans

Clever Hans was a horse who, according to his owner, could count. If you called the horse an addition task, for example 3 + 4, then it stomped seven times with the hoof on the ground. This not only worked with the owner, but also when strangers set the tasks. After many speculations and publications especially by experts, it turned out that the clever Hans had learned to interpret the tension of the respective person before the number of results and relaxation in this number. These motor utterances are usually not even aware of humans. They were mainly described by Paul Ekman (see Bibliography).

If someone says "My dog can read minds" ... then the dog simply reads the motor signals, among other things. And, as studies show, these motor signals often appear before consciousness.

For example, your facial expressions and your body say "sit" before you even thought it, let alone said it.

The "clever Hans trauma" of psychology has led among other things to the methodology of double-blind studies, in which none of the interaction partners knows the solution. We will come back to the meaning of body language and facial expressions.

The social interaction with humans is rather strenuous for dogs, in contrast to the interaction in the dog pack, since it decodes the signs of humans in the form of body language and facial expressions. Therefore, dogs also need enough rest and breaks from social interaction with humans.

The situation is similar with autistics due to the lack of unconscious group interaction. The phonetic language (in contrast to the body language) of NT people consists of about 60% "grooming", ie unconscious group communication, and only about 40% of factual information. But only this factual information is of interest to autistics, can be understood by them at all. Filtering out the modest amount of factual information from the overall package of NT communication requires a lot of practice and energy from autistics.

In addition, filtering out, for example, the language against background noise, which goes hand in hand with a high energy expenditure due to the lack of stimulus filter. Autistic people also need regeneration phases again and again in order to build up energy again.

Therefore, when interacting with both autistic people and dogs, clear and concise verbal communication is preferable to being extravagant. In dogs, one can even do without verbal communication to a large extent, if one controls nonverbal communication through body language and gestures. In any case, but a short "sit" is far more promising than a "Oh my sweatheart, please come here to me and sit down". And also the repetition of a command, if this is not carried out immediately by the dog, makes little sense. Because as a rule, the non-compliance is not because your dog has not heard you or has not understood the command, but the dog does not take it seriously. For example, when it comes to food, your dog will hear you in the last corner and hurry up immediately. Just give it a try - you'll be amazed how well your dog can "hear".

When communicating with autistic people, speech communication should at least be significantly reduced in relation to communication with NT people, who always expect a large proportion of relationship communication. And that too, for example, to provide autistic children with space for their utterances. Often, when a child does not speak, a vicious circle arises, in which the parents, on the one hand, speak more and more and, on the other hand, do more and more in anticipatory obedience to the child.

On the one hand there is hardly any room for the child's utterances in the spoken language - and on the other hand, it does not need it, as it receives everything it needs, even without speaking. Just like dogs too, which the owners often read every wish from the lips.

A fallacy similar to that the reason for not following a command is that the dog has not heard or understood this command is the misconception that mutant children just do not understand spoken language just because they do not speak.

1.3   Pack, ranking and orientation

In dogs, there is still a pack animal due to the descent of the wolf. This is often forgotten because we can hardly experience dogs in pack anymore. And we humans are much more "pack animals", act largely unconscious and group-dependent, as we want to admit this.

The results of social psychology in recent decades, however, speak a clear language regarding the group dependence of human behavior.

If you can watch a dog pack, it quickly becomes clear that dogs are much more robust in dealing with each other than we humans imagine. Dogs are less prudish about greeting, playing, and negotiating the order of rank within the pack, as we usually do with them!

On the other hand, there are rules in the pack and also limits in the interaction. If this limit of one dog is exceeded by another, this is indicated for example by a short squeak, after which the other dog usually ceases or at least reduces its behavior.

For dogs, the social structure within the pack also provides an important orientation.

For modern people, at least intellectually, an orientation towards the group, and to that an unconscious one, is almost unthinkable to think and accept.

Despite the results of social psychology.

The ideas of freedom, individuality and equality have shaped our ideas too much. This masking (unconscious) group behavior often leads to problems in both the education of children and dogs.

1.3.a   Excursus: Survival Strategies

Life is a process that, under the expense of energy, runs counter to entropy. Entropy is the term for a process that causes things usually to assume a state of maximum disorder because it has the lowest energy level.

We are surrounded by many such processes.

So the apartment becomes completely dirty by itself, the flowers wither, if we do not pour them. Not only we are aging, but also our dog, and the bread rots in the bread box ...

So life means the ongoing struggle against the process of

decay by using energy.

To ensure survival, some basic strategies are found on living beings in general.

Above all, it is the search for food (energy) and (sexual) propagation. In order to secure these processes, there are added as "auxiliary services", without claim to completeness:

- Exploratory behavior. The environment is explored over and over again to find food sources and sexual partners.

- Aggression - to defend territory, food and sexual partners against competitors, and to defend themselves as well as the brood against predators.

- Stress - as a physiological response to a threat to equip the body for flight or fight.

- Social behavior - to enable survival in a group.

All auxiliary services are so first of all "normal" and serve life. Not only social behavior, but also aggression and exploration behavior. But the latter two have, wrongly, a bad reputation, seem to stand in the way of social behavior.

Just as a dog literally has to stick his nose in everything because of his exploration behavior, so you can often see it in autistic people. Of course, limits are also necessary here, not everything should be sniffed by the dog, not everything has to be explored by the child. But often we at the Solidar Hotel have the impression that due to social conventions, the limits of the exploratory behavior of (autistic) children are far too narrow. But both children and dogs need the opportunity to explore their surroundings. And as a child, literally "manipulating" this environment - touching, feeling, dropping things ...

These manipulations of the environment, the opening of cabinet doors etc. are an important part of learning. Often we experience how parents limit their autistic children's exploratory behavior, preventing exploration instead of using it as a starting point for social interaction. So instead of exploring the environment together, for example.

But also aggression has its firm place in the behavior of animal and humans, as long as it remains limited. Not the aggression as such is bad, just an unlimited, exuberant one.

The help services can also occur in various combinations.

For example, the game is often a combination of exploration and (playful) aggression!

Bullying in its original form, described by Konrad Lorenz in the animal kingdom as "Hassen", is aggression in combination with social behavior when, for example, predators are attacked and driven out together. In humans, on the other hand, the bullying gets out of hand - and often catastrophic consequences for the culled man.

At the same time, however, the individual is always in conflict between the pursuit of his own goals and those of his own group. So between egoism and altruism, between "me" and "we".

Here, through social interaction, it is important to learn the limits of, for example, aggressive behavior within the group.

Testing boundaries in behavior towards others is part of exploration behavior.

If the physical environment is normally explored, then in this case it is the social structure (of the group). Testing borders also helps to learn social (!) interaction.

And if the recurring "questions" about the competencies of others and one's own position within the social structure are not answered, two problems arise.

For one thing, social behavior is not developed. Because

social interaction is learned above all through one thing: through social interaction.

But if the boundaries for the behavior of the individual within the group are not shown, this is synonymous with the denial of social (!) interaction.

For example, the hunting and barking of a jogger by a dog is an interaction - but not a social one.

Social interaction is defined by considering the boundaries and needs of the other participants in the interaction.

On the other hand, children as well as dogs who are not clearly identified with boundaries develop the "idea" that they are the "bosses" of the family or the pack.

That would not be too bad if children and dogs were not completely overwhelmed by leadership within a human family. If it does not require skills that they are not capable of. Instead of providing them with orientation, even through clearly defined boundaries that they need.

1.4   Ambivalence of boundaries

Borders have two faces. For one thing, they can narrow and hinder you. On the other hand, they also give security and orientation. Culturally conditioned, only the negative sides of borders are perceived, a world without borders is dreamed. The positive aspects of borders and their necessity are often overlooked.

Borders provide a framework in which one can develop freely and safely. Yes, borders are, to a degree, a prerequisite for freedom. Therefore, borders are important for both children and dogs.

The greatest freedom for a dog, free running without a leash, requires that the dog obeys. And not a bit obeys in the sense "Come here or let it stay," but reliably follows the command. Without this obedience, the dog without a leash would not only be a danger to joggers, cyclists ... but also to himself, if he were, for example. walking on a busy road.

Border means "to this point, and not further!".

A modern misconception in both the child and dog training is to be able to communicate these boundaries only by positive reinforcement, ie by the gift of "treat", and / or ignoring the border violations.

It overlooks the fact that exploring boundaries based on exploration behavior is an automatic and recurrent process - in children and dogs.

And the clearer the answer to the asked "question" about the border, the more effective it will be.

If the necessary (!) boundaries are not set clearly, if a transgression is ignored and not punished, then that means that the questions about the position within the social structure are not answered. Both children and dogs "swim" without consistently formulated and enforced borders.

They are then in a permanent state of demand, exploration and testing. For this, on the one hand, a lot of energy is needed, on the other hand, the children and dogs are then, so to speak, in a "vacuum", in uncertainty. It lacks the possibility of orientation to competent interaction partners within the social structure.

And so it comes to a reversal of the orientation direction. No more child or dog orients themselves to the adult, but vice versa.

1.4.a   Exkursus: Orientation

As a result of the 1968s, much was wrongly discredited in Germany, especially the natural (!) authority due to competence. If one asks the question, who should be guided by whom, then the simple answer is: the less competent by the more competent. The idea of equality, that is, the same claim to the development of personality, was confused with egalitarianism.

But unfortunately it is so that my dog does not iron my shirts, not stroking my belly, but only me him. That

Krishna, such a super good dog he is, does not pay the rent and buy the food.

Dogs generally do not know the rules of living together, but they have to be taught to them, as well as children. This mediation takes place through social interaction in which the (hopefully) more competent person sets the direction and sets limits. And so that the less experienced, less competent, can orient themselves to it.

Autistic children in particular, who find it particularly difficult to find their bearings due to the lack of an "autopilot", need clear structures and boundaries - not for narrowing down - but for orientation.

1.5   Exercise

Already in the book "Support for Autistic?" [Schmidt, B.J. 2015/2)], the default mode and task mode were displayed in detail. It was also stated that autistics are missing the default mode, which is mainly responsible for the unconscious group behavior, and they are therefore predominantly in task mode. This is associated with a high level of activity, a strong need for movement and, if not restricted by fear, with strong exploration behavior. A common misinterpretation of autistic children is the "runaway tendency", which in many cases is

simply a "running trend" due to the high level of activity.
And even dogs, except a few breeds, need a lot of
exercise.

Practical example : T.

Running is T.s (18 years old and Asperger) great passion.
Whenever he came out of his room, it was only passing
by the other guests and taking long trips to the forest. T.
was very sporty on the one hand, on the other hand very
withdrawn at first. He largely avoided leaving the room
and being in contact with people. After a few days with
us, we could identify his withdrawal not as a symptom of
autism, but as a social phobia. Subsequent intervention
gradually eliminated this phobia.
Unfortunately we did not have Krishna at the time when
T. was our guest. It would have been exciting if a
relationship between the athlete T. and the former sled
dog Krishna had developed. Whether T. was pleased
about the accompaniment of Krishna during his walks
and felt this enrichment.
But T. would like to visit the Solidar Hotel again.
Then there will be an opportunity to provide T. a dog
(Krishna) as a guide on his excursions.

1.6   Between education and dressage

Unfortunately, a common feature between autistic children and dogs is that there are quite a few people who see and treat them as mere stimulus-response machines. The possibilities of conditioning and behaviorism seem to exert a very strong attraction today. And that although or perhaps because life is much more complex than a stimulus-response mechanism.

In the context of autistic children, this view is expressed in the form of, for example, ABA, the "applied behavioral analysis" that seeks to strengthen desired behavior by rewarding and, in the past, punishment, and to discourage unwanted behavior.

In dogs, it is the attempt of a relationship building on treats - which is ultimately ABA for dogs.

Both works only very limited. On the one hand, the results are often neither permanent, on the other hand, the learning outcomes are often not transferable.

Dog owners, who have managed to train their dogs to their leashes through their treats in a familiar environment, are suddenly dealing with non-leashed dogs in other surroundings.

But, of course, dogs are, to a degree, stimulus-response machines. And people, whether autistic or not, are too.

But the totality of their being can not be understood that way.

Limiting the perspective, in both autistic and dog, purely on the stimulus-response behavior, stands in the way of building, developing and promoting social interaction! It should not be overlooked that not only humans, but also animals can develop strategies that reach far beyond stimulus-response behavior (see Bibliography: Sommer, Volker: Lob der Lüge).

A sustainable social relationship can not be built purely by means of dressage.

A stable interaction that goes far beyond the stimulus-response scheme also works especially when the environment changes or the treat bag is forgotten. But how is a stable and sustainable relationship achieved? By education instead of dressage.

Education guides learning and exploration based on competence and limits aggression.

Dressage, on the other hand, trains desired "tricks" and trains off unwanted behavior.

Education, on the other hand, also leads, through social interaction, to the mediation of necessary boundaries in the context of coexistence and thus social behavior.

Education should therefore be based on social interaction and aimed at building trust. But it also takes place in a social environment of expectations, conventions and values ... and people are not only unsure about dog training.

It should not be overlooked in education that not only the adult educates the child or the dog, but also the child and the dog educate the adult. Both sides are in a social interaction circle of mutual influence and the development of chains of action. Both children and dogs have the capacity for strategic manipulation to achieve survival.

And only the interaction that respects the nature and peculiarities of the counterpart is social and promotes the development of both human and dog.

One should be aware that children and dogs ALWAYS learn, observe and try to draw conclusions from the observed ... and not only when we want to teach them something. An essential part of education is therefore our role model of social interaction with others.

2   Encouraging interaction = promoting development

The other form of perception as well as communication with autistic people carries two risks. On the one hand, it is anxiety and stress that can arise either from the sensory overload or the lack of orientation on the group. On the

other hand, it is not uncommon for the interaction with the environment to be disrupted, as a result of which a development of the autistic child may be disrupted. Because development needs interaction!
Autism is therefore not a "profound developmental disorder", but a special perception and communication that can lead to a disruption of social interaction and - as a result - to a disruption of development.
Thus it becomes clear that the restoration or improvement of the social interaction with the autistic person should be a central goal. Dogs can be very helpful here.

3   Anxiety and stress as obstacles

Fear and stress are the main obstacles to building a social interaction - whether between humans or humans and dogs.
With his "Polyvagal Theory" Stephen Porges (see Bibliography) describes very impressively the evolutionary developments that have led to mammals only being able to interact socially if they perceive the environment as safe.
This is nicely expressed in the headline to an article by Ravi Dykema on the Polyvagal theory: "Do not talk to me now, I'm scanning for danger" [Dykema (2006)].

As long as a mammal is in escape or combat mode, it can not interact socially.

But since social interaction is the essential prerequisite for development, anxiety and stress stand in the way of not only social interaction, but also the development of autistic children.

How quickly autistic children can develop in a friendly and sensory low-threshold environment, which is perceived by the children as "safe", we experience again and again in the Solidar Hotel. So far, and we are quite proud of this, no family with an autistic child had to cancel their holiday with us. On the contrary, many autistic children and adolescents wanted to stay right here with us or at least spend their holidays with us again. This shows how great the influence of the environment can be on the development of autistic people in both good and bad.

The previous and still widespread focus solely on the autistic is far too short and runs past the target.

IV. GOALS

The most important goal when buying a dog should be to enjoy being with it.

Who does not enjoy working with dogs, who, for example, long walks with the dog can gain nothing, so who only hopes to improve the behavior of the autistic child, should refrain from the purchase of a dog.

Beyond this joy of being together with a dog, however, the following aims can and should be pursued.

1   Reduction of anxiety and stress

It has already been shown that anxiety and stress are major barriers to social interaction and thus to the development of autistic children.

Thus, the reduction of anxiety and stress should be one of the essential objectives of the acquisition of a dog.

Dogs are very well able to cope with this reduction in anxiety and stress when the conditions of dog ownership, for example, are right. This is proven by several studies.

Not only can dogs "read" our body language, they also smell our mood.

Dogs, for example, are able to perceive our cortisol levels (cortisol is a stress hormone) via the sense of smell and can thus smell our stress level. But also joy, sadness and many other emotions can be perceived by dogs, and behave according to us. If the interaction between man and dog is right, then the affection of a dog is always perfect and unconditional. It is not without reason that people say that nobody is as reliable a friend as a dog. At the same time, a dog is also a companion, ally and protector, and can also reduce anxiety and stress. And not only with the autistic child or adolescent, but with the whole family.

Practical example : Gismo
Gismo, a 10-year-old former street dog, has learned to shield his owner from crowds on command. At the commands "before" or "behind" he stands in front of or behind his owner and shields her from other people in a crowd, for example at a Christmas market.

2 Promotion of social interaction (Catalyst)

As we will discuss in more detail in the chapter on our experiences with autistic children and their parents and siblings in the dog school, the interaction between parent and dog as well as child and dog can also contribute to

improving the interaction between parents and (autistic) child.
This should also be the goal of a dog in the family.
The dog acts as a kind of catalyst for the social interaction between the parents and the autistic child, as shown in the diagram. In this case, the vertical position also reflects the position within the family structure. With the parents at the top (hopefully agreeing on education issues), followed by the child or children, and then the dog.

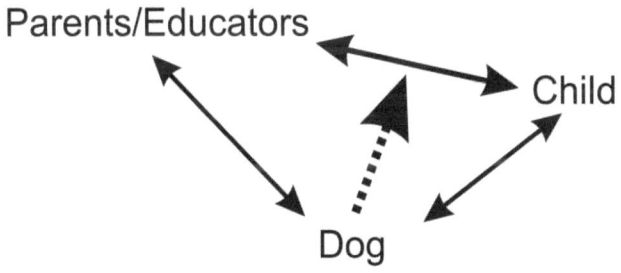

Unfortunately, one can always observe other constructions and above all rankings between man and dog.
All other conceivable constellations of social structure also occur - with correspondingly different problems.

3   Abuse of a dog

However, a dog can also be used not to promote interaction with one's own child, but to restrict and hinder it.

In an internet video, a father is shown who has trained a dog as a kind of "herding dog" for his autistic son. The dog gets, for example the son back when it has "run away" and lies down at the bus stop on the legs of the child, so that the child can not move. Otherwise, the autistic boy is tied to the leash of the dog and must follow the dog, which is led by the father.

This only works "sweet" because the "chain" to which the child hangs is a dog. But it is just as cruel as if the child were really being dragged along a chain.

Because the interaction takes place only between father and dog, and no longer with the child.

But without social interaction, the development is at least disturbed.

At the same time the child is robbed of the freedom, for example, by the dog lays down on the legs of the child, and also the radius of the child is limited by the leash.

Instead of promoting social interaction between parents and children, the dog is abused to avoid them. By preventing the interaction between father and son, the development of the child is at least hindered, if not prevented.

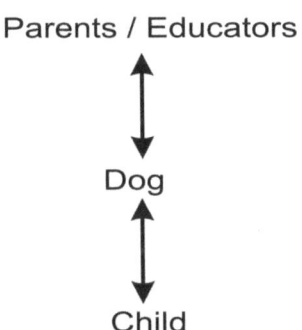

The interaction is no longer between parent and child, but is delegated to the dog.

At the same time, the child is placed on a hierarchical level to which it does not belong.

Both make the development of the autistic child difficult if not impossible.

This is only understandable by the fact that the autism research of the past 50 years has given parents the wrong (!) information that the autistic children can not develop, never develop and are to be regarded as pure stimulus-response machines.

It is a major failure of autism research to deny autistic children a decades-long developmental perspective that understands social interaction as the foundation and necessary precondition for potential development.

V. PRACTICE

Probably the most important difference in the interaction with a dog is the question of whether one tries to motivate or condition it by the permanent gift of "treat". Or if you try to build a real relationship between dog and human.

In the "treat" variant, which is also found in many, if not most, dog training schools today, man turns himself into a pure food donor. And should not be surprised if he is perceived by the dog even so.

On the other hand, the goal is a successful and intensive social interaction between man and dog. For us, the "treat" method is out of the question. And this on the one hand in principle, on the other hand, but also because of the goal of promoting social interaction between, for example, autistic and dog.

The difference becomes clear when you use a bag of treats. If the person is equipped with this, the dog only pays attention to the bag, orients itself to it. Without food bags, the dog is based on humans.

This does not mean that a reward in the form of a treat can be useful and even necessary. But it should not be the basic principle of human-dog interaction.

And of course not the basis of interaction between people, whether autistic or not.

1   Purchase of a dog

A dog should never be just a means, for example the to improve social interaction within the family, but always also its own purpose. As a living thing, a dog has its own needs and rights.

In the beginning, the question should be whether one can meet the needs of a dog at all. Whether the temporal and other circumstances within the family allow the welfare of a dog at all. Which race could be suitable for the given possibilities.

A dog also causes a considerable amount of time and costs, which can quickly exceed the cost of purchase. All this should be considered in advance to avoid problems and disappointments. Because the stress level is often high enough in families with autistic children, and should actually be reduced by a dog and not increased.

Practical example: Th.
The parents of Th., 21 years old and mutist autistic thought about the acquisition of a dog. Through the consultation, it turned out that both parents went to work and there was little time to work with a dog. Also, the

goal of an acquisition was just to get a positive effect on Th. A dog as such was intended only as a means of doing so.

1.1   Does the child react to a dog?

If you are positive about the acquisition of a dog in principle - not only as a means to an end - then it should be clarified in advance, if the autistic child even reacts to a dog. Although many children generally have a good relationship with dogs - but not all.

Practical example: R.
When visiting the dog school, R., 4 years and mutist autistic, showed no interest in the dogs. He preferred to play with the water tanks available there. Also on another visit the dogs were not of direct interest to R. We will come back to it.

It is therefore advisable to use other means of contact with dogs before purchasing a dog, for example a dog school, animal shelter or a therapist with a therapy dog. Animal shelters often offer the possibility to rent a dog for "go for a walk".
This will avoid disappointment if the child does not

respond to the newly purchased dog as one would have liked.

Practical example: L.

The opposite of R. (see above) was L., 6 years old and mutist autistic. Although L. normally walked around the area with a blank, expressionless gaze, also through the guest rooms of the Solidar Hotel, she blossomed fully in the presence of the dogs. She smiled and was happy, made eye contact, and looked around.

But even if the autistic child does not react positively to a dog, it can make sense to buy it. For one thing, building a relationship between the autistic and the dog sometimes just takes a bit longer. And on the other hand, dogs can not only have a positive effect on the autistic children and adolescents, but on the entire family.

1.2   What kind of dog?

If, after hopefully careful consideration, you have decided to buy a dog, you must clarify the question of what kind of dog should become part of the family. Every dog breed has its own needs and advantages. Even if the dogs of one breed can be very different, there is a basic tendency. Some races are more human-oriented and social-interactive than others. Some need more exercise, challenge and activity than others ...

In the end, the dog should not fit the family in terms of appearance or fashion, but rather by its nature and needs. It is best to seek competent and independent advice (ie neither from breeders, dog dealers or "normal" dog owners) before purchasing a dog. The advice of a qualified dog trainer especially regarding the breed can save a lot of trouble.

Not only in Internet forums one finds again and again "autism assistance dogs" advertised. But does it have to be one?

Unlike, for example, in the blind, where the guide dog must take on important tasks that require a lengthy training, the dog is used in families with autistic children or adult autistic especially the two points of stress reduction and social interaction. Although it is helpful if the dog is related to people and already educated. But the need to build a sustainable relationship through social interaction is not eliminated. This build-up of the relationship must be done by the buyers themselves, through many hours of social interaction.

The main advantage of trained assistance dogs is perhaps that the willingness to acquire necessary skills for dog ownership is higher in a dog that costs several thousand euros, as a dog from the shelter. But miracles can not even cause trained assistance dogs, at least in the area of autism. The time-consuming main task of social interaction with the dog is and will not be spared the (future) owners.

1.3 No helper syndrome (stray dogs)

The rescue of stray dogs is currently a big topic. But are former stray dogs suitable for families with autistic children?
Considering the already high stress levels in these families, plus the often not very large time reserves for an intensive activity with the dog, one has to negate this question rather.
The goal of purchasing a dog is above all the reduction of stress - not the construction of new ones.
Through life on the street, these dogs are often geared not to humans, but rather to the struggle for survival by all means.

Practical example: L.
The family of L., Asperger and 10 years old, had two street dogs rescued in Eastern Europe. These were, like stray dogs often, very lively and independent.
In addition, the education of the two dogs, despite the

several months of visiting a dog school left a lot to be desired.
For example, a relaxed walk on a leash with the two dogs was not possible.
L. was a total Krishna fan, even though there were two dogs in the family, and he always wanted to cuddle with Krishna.
The big difference in the nature as well as the education of the dogs makes this easy to understand.

This does not mean that rescued street dogs can never be suitable for families with autistic children. There is nothing against the purchase of a former street dog, if enough time and energy is available. On the one hand to acquire the necessary skills for the leadership of a street dog (if not available), and on the other hand to train and challenge the dog accordingly. Yes, interacting with stray dogs can be even more exciting.

Practical example: Ti.
The two former stray dogs of Ti., 29 years old and Asperger, are the opposite of the dogs of L.
Stray dogs are usually hardly influenced by humans and at the same time selected for a hard struggle for survival.
Nevertheless, the two dogs of Ti. are two well behaved (street) dogs, which are also well suited for interaction

with children due to a high temporal commitment in terms of training and education. Nevertheless, they are very demanding.

In principle, it is not recommended to buy several dogs at the beginning. Before the purchase of a second dog, there should be no problems with the leadership of the first dog.

No problem in dealing with the first dog can be solved by the purchase of a second dog - on the contrary.

1.3.a Age of the dog

Puppies are so cute. But it should not be forgotten that the education of a puppy takes a lot of time and nerves. Time that should be better invested in promoting the autistic child. It would therefore be worth considering whether one would rather acquire an older, already trained dog. It does not necessarily have to be an expensive assistance dog. There are always well-trained dogs like our Krishna, who "retire" in their previous job and are looking forward to a new job in a family. For example dogs originally intended as guide dogs, or raised by breeders but not suitable for breeding ... The effort to find a suitable dog is certainly worthwhile.

1.3.b   What should the dog be able to do?

People often put a lot of emphasis on mastery of tricks in dogs, even if it's just "giving a paw". For the good, stress-reducing and social interaction-promoting coexistence with a dog, such tricks, as entertaining as they may be, are irrelevant.
Much more important, however, is the "social competence" of the dog. A dog should therefore bring along the following characteristics if possible:

–   Shaped on people and interested in social interaction with people. That means no very independent breeds like terriers, herding dogs, nordic and asian breeds.

–   Compatible with children

–   Compatible with other dogs / animals

–   Controllable or no hunting behavior

–   Resistant to stress

–   Obedience (Leashes, Basic Commands ...)

Tricks or even commands such as placing in front of or behind the autists can then still be taught to the dog. Some races are better, others less. Because the education of the dog always builds on the genetic predisposition.

1.4   How do I lead a dog?

To lead a dog is no child's play. A dog is a living being, should be sensitive and able to learn - and can therefore be "corrupted" by wrong treatment. Unfortunately, it takes a lot longer to educate a dog than to turn it into a "problem dog".

And even the maximum trained, a few thousand euro expensive assistance dog is not resistant to wrong guidance by its owner. Thus, if not already sufficiently existent, with the acquisition of a dog, the appropriate appropriation of the necessary knowledge and skills in dog handling should go hand in hand.

Otherwise, there is a high risk that the dog will cause more stress than breaking it down after a few weeks.

The fact that the visit of a suitable dog school not only conveys the necessary abilities regarding the dog, but can also positively change the social interaction between autistic child and parents, we were allowed to experience again and again in the last months.

Suitable are dog training schools, which attach particular

importance to the establishment of a stable social relationship between humans and dogs, which use barely treats and clickers, and do not believe that the misconduct of the dog should be treated in principle with ignoring. This can be useful in some cases - but not as a universal solution.

VI. EXPERIENCES FROM THE DOG SCHOOL

Once a week, the families at the Solidar Hotel Goldener Stern can visit the dog school located within walking distance. Already here the difference to the previous perspective becomes clear on the interaction between autistic child and dog.

Because not only the autistic children attend the dog school. On the one hand, the entire family of the autistic child, including the siblings, usually comes along. On the other hand, families with neurotypical children also participate.

This is possible because the dog school also belongs to a dog breed. In this European sled dogs are bred and reared, and not for sale, but especially for their own needs.

So there are always at least 8 dogs with similar training levels and pronounced social behavior available. This allows each family to get "their" dog for the training lesson to practice with.

Since all dogs enjoy being with each other, as well as commanding and interacting with people, problems with human-dog interaction always have their cause in the individual who guides the dog.

So if the dog does not understand what the individual wants from him, then it is clearly a problem in human communication. This is particularly interesting in the context of the interaction with autistic individuals, as the causes of "disruption of interaction" over 50 years have been attributed to autistic individuals alone.

But at least in the interaction with the trained dogs shows that problems can also be present on the part of parents and siblings.

1   Changing the focus

The handling of the dogs shifts the attention of the parents very strongly during the training hour. In many families, all attention is almost always on the autistic child.

However, this also means, albeit without intention, that the range of action of the child is very severely restricted and that all activities are "monitored". Thus, even normal and ultimately very desirable exploration behavior, ie the exploration of the environment, for example by running into our kitchen, is frequently suppressed.

By working with the dogs, the attention of the parents is now deducted from the children, because it is claimed by the dogs.

This always leads to the fact that the autistic children can use this, at one time available, free space.

Practical example: L.

For the dogs, L., 6 years old, little and ritualized speaking early childhood autistic, hardly cared. The tunnel for the dogs, through which they must run as an exercise, had attracted L.'s attention. The parents were busy with the dogs, so he could crawl through the tunnel again and again. Praised for it, he then celebrated himself every new round with a cheerful "tunnel!".

Development needs limits, but also needs free space. By focusing completely on the autistic child, it is often taken away from the space necessary for exploration and development.

Through the experience in the dog school, parents often learn quickly that it is good to allow the child also freedoms and to turn the attention even once from the child.

1.1   Offering competition

The dogs are at once a competition to the child. The child is suddenly no longer at the center of attention of the parents, but the interaction with the dogs. The one children use this freedom, as previously described, while others try to regain the parents' attention immediately. And usually by shouting.

Practical example: R.

During an individual lesson we left the area together with the parents and two dogs. The autistic child, R. 4-year-old mutist autist, stopped at the gate and screamed. However, as both the dogs and we stayed calm, it was also possible for the parents to stay calm.
Quite quickly, the child realized that it can not enforce his will and parents will not rush to the child. So the child came to us, sought contact with the parents, and no longer demanded this dominant. This interaction, lasting only a few minutes, at least temporarily restored a natural orientation. The child followed the parents and not the other way round.

Giving children the clear orientation they need is not evil but necessary.
Unfortunately, our cultural perception has developed in a different direction.

1.2   Interesting activity of the parents

By focusing all attention on the autistic child and his desires, not only will his or her development be limited, but also opportunities for parents to develop. However, exciting activities of the parents in combination with the shift of attention can be quite interesting for the autistic child and lead to social interaction.

Practical example: R.
As stated earlier, R., 4 years old and mutist autistic, initially had no interest in the dogs. This remained so with another visit. However, the parents did not allow their child to distract them from working with the dogs. As a result, after some time, R. became interested in caring for his parents and running to his parents.

Interaction means looking at each other. Interesting activities of the parents can be an invitation for the children to be interested in the parents and their activities and to orient themselves towards the parents.

2   Praise and reward

Often the parents of autistic children only perceive the
negative characteristics and behavior of the children.
Positive behaviors and developments, on the other hand,
are often overlooked.
Negative beliefs that autistic children can not do or
understand such things often stand in the way of
promoting development. And so, the positive behaviors
that show autistic children, on the one hand often
overlooked, on the other hand, of course, not appreciated
accordingly. But recognition, praise and reward is
important for everyone, for both humans and dogs. By
working with the dogs, by the necessary praise of the dog
after a successful exercise, the parents are reminded again
to praise their children for progress and successful
actions. For why should the child do something when the
environment does not matter? How can the child
recognize that it did something right?
And why should the child make an effort if success is
ignored?
And praise and reward can also be expressed through
treats - but they do not have to be. This is where verbal
praise, a joyful celebration of success often suffice, as are
the basic components of child-centered support programs

61

such as AuJA and Son-Rise®.

In the absence of praise and attention in the case of positive behavior, children and even dogs quickly learn that they receive the required attention very reliably, at least in the event of misconduct.

3   Clear communication

The dogs used in the dog school are all "leashed", so they follow the leash.

At the beginning of the lesson, however, the new, unknown person at the other end of the leash is more of an annoying obstacle. The other dogs on the field, the owner and passing cars ... everything is more interesting than the unknown person at the other end of the leash.

So you can often observe in the beginning that people follow the dog and not the dog to the person.

Therefore, the first exercise that people usually do is communicate with the dog.

And that they make it clear to the dog that the dog should focus on them and be guided by them.

People should start a "conversation" with the dog, a social interaction. The goal is for the leash to become a "telephone wire", ie a means of communication between human and dog. The most important prerequisite for this is that the leash is not tense but loose. So that you can theoretically hold the leash with two fingers and the dog follows anyway. Alone, many dog owners are far away, but they follow the dog rather than the dog on their leash. But even a dog that is "leashed", the human must clearly communicate what the dog should do so he can do it. If a person does not know what he wants and / or communicates vaguely, the interaction with the dog will be difficult if not impossible.

Especially at the beginning it is difficult to get the attention of the dog at all. And if you get them by calling or nudging - then usually only for a few seconds. Timing is everything. If I ask the dog's attention, then I should know what I want. And on the other hand, communicate this immediately and clearly. Otherwise, the dog's attention is either back on other things. Or if I do not clearly communicate what I want, he does not understand me.

However, many mistakes that are often made when communicating with dogs can be corrected relatively quickly.

3.1   Facial expressions and body language

NT people put too much emphasis on the spoken language. Among other things, this is due to the importance of unconscious group orientation and the

accompanying small-talk as social "grooming".
As a result, dog owners are often inclined to "chatting away" their dogs.
But dogs are more geared to our body language and facial expressions than to the spoken language.
Am I bowed or upright? Do I bend over the dog, in which direction do I go, in which direction do I look ...?

Practical example:
The dog trainer explained to man-trailing, the search for people, the target people the place to go and hide there. The dog then also led the dog trainer to this point. Only the target persons had misunderstood the description and were elsewhere. The dog had therefore not followed the track of the target persons, but had based on the body language of the dog trainer.

The body language, our facial expressions and gestures are much more important to the dog than the spoken language. And can also lead to major irritations. Do I still scowl because I still think about the argument at work while rewarding my dog? Or maybe I look quite happy as I scold my dog for hunting because the freedom-loving hunter in me secretly calls the dog's behavior good.

3.1.a   Excursus: Schulz von Thun and the "inner team"

People tend to perceive themselves as a psychic entity. As a rule, as Schulz von Thun describes in detail in his book "Miteinander reden, Band 3", a person does not consist of a single personality, but of many internal currents and desires, of different personalities - the "inner team". Each of these sides, each current has a different direction, different values, goals ...

For example, a member of the team could be the freedom fighter and daredevil. Another the fearful, who fears losses. Added to this is perhaps the animal rights activist, who cares about the welfare of the animals. And the law-abiding, for which the observance of all rules is of great importance.

If the dog of the owner, who carries all these different inner attitudes, hunts, different voices will be announced in the holder and the hunting will be judged differently. The freedom fighter and daredevil will sanctify it secretly.

The animal rights activist cares about the hunted deer. Although the deer does not care for the timid, he fears that the dog will not come back after his hunting trip or is shot dead by the hunter.

And the law-abiding annoys the violation of the rules.

So what will be the reaction to the hunting behavior of the dog?

The freedom fighter wants to praise the dog, the timid rejoice over the return, the animal rights activists scold the dog - but not too strong, and the lawfulness punish the dog for his offense.

All of these actions compete with each other and will be reflected in both the minespiel and the behavior of the owner (if he has not previously become aware of these currents). This creates a message for the dog that the dog can not decipher.

In addition to facial expressions, the (correct) body language is also important for communication with the dog.

It seems unfamiliar to humans, but if I want the dog to follow me, then I will walk away from it - and not towards it.

As an exercise, this means calling for the dog's attention. And as soon as the dog looks, turn around and walk away. So an invitation to the dog is expressed to follow one.

And even if a strange dog comes running up and you (out

of fear) runs away, this dog feels that as an invitation to run afterwards. If the human also raises his arms, this is understood by the dog even more as an invitation to jump up.

So if I want the dog to come to me, I'll call him and not walk towards him, but away from him. If I want the opposite, namely that the dog dodges me, then I go to the dog.

3.2   Eye contact / viewing direction

Eye contact is overrated especially in the western world. The entire autism research is permeated by the obsession that one must look other people in the eye. But in other cultures as well as in dogs, the look in the eyes partly causes the opposite of a friendly contact. The look in the eyes can be understood as aggression: "What are you looking at ?!".

Dogs are also oriented to the line of sight of humans. It follows that you should not look at the dog, but look in the direction you want to go. It is precisely this behavior that makes it particularly difficult for NT people to do the exercises. They always look at the dogs instead of the direction they want to go.

The look to other people probably serves the unconscious orientation to the group, so it is more of a question than an instruction. Instead of a "we go in this direction" so the question to the group "Is it okay if we go in this direction?". But this is a question that neither dog nor autist can understand, let alone answer, in this unconscious form of group interaction.

4   Strengthening siblings

Often the needs of the siblings of autistic children are neglected, especially those of the sisters. They often have a very high level of social skills and are very focused on making everything right for their autistic siblings as well as their parents. Own wishes and needs are often put back.
The opportunity to have a dog for yourself during the training hour and to work with it also gives the siblings the opportunity to perceive their own wishes and goals, at least in this area. And also to learn to communicate them clearly, and to enforce them against the dog. When working with a dog, as already explained, the orientation towards the group, in this case to the needs of the others, no longer works.

VII.   SUMMARY

Dogs can be very conducive to social interaction within a family with an autistic child.
On the one hand by the reduction of stress, on the other hand by the special way of communication with a dog. These positive consequences of the purchase of a dog, however, presupposed

- the correct selection of the dog in terms of race and training,

- a species-appropriate dog ownership,

- and to guide the dog competently!

It should be expected no miracles, but it should be the joy of dealing and social interaction with a dog in the foreground.
The interaction with a dog can sometimes be compared to a game of chess. Each move of the one player is the requirement and creates the conditions for the next move of the other player.
Everybody interprets the behavior of the other person in his own way. These interpretations in turn are the basis

for one's own actions. And you should enjoy the game of chess, as well as being with a dog. The capabilities and strategies of a dog are much more far-reaching than many assumptions of learning theory suggest, which have their justification within a certain scope.

If you treat your dog with treats, clicks, and / or ignorance (towards unwanted behavior), then you will interact with a stimulus-response machine. But that's not the dog, it's your interpretation of its behavior and the behavior that you derive from it.

Practical example: Ti. and Krishna

Krishna and I accompanied Ti., 29, and Asperger for a conversation at a counseling center.

Although Ti has two dogs of his own, we chose Krishna as a companion dog.

On the way to the consulting room, the counseling center shows Ti's tense by taking the leash way too short, almost on the collar. And that against better knowledge. Due to the leash, Krishna did not orient himself to me as usual, but to Ti.

The feedback from me that Ti takes the leash far too short, she was aware of their own tension.

During the counseling session, Ti Krishna "tickles" quite hard - just like you scratch a dog when you're under stress. Also, I pointed out to Ti.

Krishna could be seen that he has not, unlike usual, the stroking enjoyed.
Nonetheless, Krishna stayed by Ti's side, allowing her to continue caressing her, even though he could have gone away or simply lay down. There was only a quick glance from Krishna to me, if everything is alright. It is these interactions that often last only fractions of a second, which can be critical to the further course of the interaction. But they also require a stable relationship and great trust between man and dog. All this can be achieved neither by treat nor clicker. These behaviors that are so often propagated today stand in the way of your most important tool - your intuition.
Only when Ti had relaxed, among other things by caressing, Krishna lay down.

Of course, the behavior of Krishna in this practical example can also be "explained" by corresponding learning theories - but you should not.
Rather, as a behavioral scientist who wants to explore the dog's abilities (for example, to deceive and lie!), you will certainly not only enjoy the many facets of your dog, but also the good social interaction with your dog.
And be your dog not only a good keeper, but also an educator who competently shows him the necessary (!)

limits. For the benefit of everyone involved in the interaction.

BIBLIOGRAPHY

1   General

Adler, Alfred: Über den nervösen Charakter (1912).
Grundzüge einer vergleichenden Individualpsychologie
und Psychotherapie.

Schulz von Thun, Friedemann (2013): Miteinander reden,
Band 3: Das "Innere Team" und situationsgerechte
Kommunikation.

Sommer, Volker (2015): Lob der Lüge. Wie in der
Evolution der Zweck die Mittel heiligt. Hirzel, S., Verlag;
1. Auflage

2   Autism

Schmidt, Bernhard J. (2015/1): Autistic and Society. An
angry Change of Perspective. Vol. I: Understanding
Autism. Norderstedt: Books on Demand.

Schmidt, Bernhard J. (2015/2): Autistic and Society. An
angry Change of Perspective. Vol. II: Support for

Autistic? Norderstedt: Books on Demand.

Schmidt, Bernhard J. (2016/1): Plaintext compact. The Asperger Syndrome – Between Bullying and Inclusion. Norderstedt: Books on Demand.

Schmidt, Bernhard J. (2016/2):
Autismus. Wenn Händewaschen hilft.
1. Auflage. Norderstedt: Books on Demand

Schmidt, Bernhard J. (2019/1): Autism and the Refrigerator Mother Myth. A Rehabilitation of Bruno Bettelheim. Norderstedt: Books on Demand.

Schmidt, Bernhard J. (2019/2): Plaintext compact. The Asperger Syndrome – for Parents. Norderstedt: Books on Demand.

Schmidt, Bernhard J. (2019/3): Plaintext compact. The Asperger Syndrome – for Teachers. Norderstedt: Books on Demand.

Schmidt, Bernhard J. (2019/4): Plaintext compact. The Asperger Syndrome – for School Assistants. Norderstedt: Books on Demand.

Schmidt, Bernhard J. (2019/5): Autism – Flight or Fight. New Perspectives on Challenging Behaviors. Norderstedt: Books on Demand.

Schmidt, Bernhard J.; Döhler, Christiane and Deniz (2018): Autism – Sexuality – Relationships. Norderstedt: Books on Demand.

Schmidt, Bernhard J.; Ganz, Andreas (2016): Plaintext compact: The Asperger Syndrome - not only for Psychotherapists. Norderstedt: Books on Demand.

Schmidt, Bernhard J.; Ganz, Andreas (2019/6): Plaintext compact. The Asperger Syndrome – for Physicians. Norderstedt: Books on Demand.

3 Dog ownership

Grewe, Michael (2010): Hunde brauchen klare Grenzen: Gesetze einer Freundschaft

4 Autistic and dogs

Berry, Alessandra, et al.: Use of Assistance and Therapy Dogs for Children with Autism Spectrum Disorders: A Critical Review of the Current Evidence

THE JOURNAL OF ALTERNATIVE AND COMPLEMENTARY MEDICINE Volume 19, Number 2, 2013, pp. 73–80 DOI: 10.1089/acm.2011.0835

Grandgeorge M, Tordjman S, Lazartigues A, Lemonnier E, Deleau M, et al. (2012): Does Pet Arrival Trigger Prosocial Behaviors in Individuals with Autism? PLoS ONE 7(8): e41739. doi:10.1371/journal.pone.0041739

Hall SS, Wright HF, Mills DS (2017): Parent perceptions of the quality of life of pet dogs living with neuro-typically developing and neuroatypically developing children: An exploratory study. PLoS ONE 12(9): e0185300. https://doi.org/10.1371/journal.pone.0185300

Solomon, O. (2010): What a Dog Can Do: Children with Autism and Therapy Dogs in Social Interaction ETHOS, Vol. 38, Issue 1, pp. 143–166, DOI: 10.1111/j.1548-1352.2009.01085.x.

Wright, H. F., et al. (2015).
Acquiring a pet dog significantly reduces stress of primary carers for children with autism spectrum disorder: A prospective case control study.
Journal of Autism and Developmental Disorders. 45(8), 2531–2540.
doi: 1 10.1007/s10803-015-2418-5.

Wright, Hannah F., et al. (2015)
Additional Evidence is Needed to Recommend Acquiring
a Dog to Families of Children with Autism Spectrum
Disorder: A Response to Crossman and Kazdin
J Autism Dev Disord
DOI 10.1007/s10803-015-2548-9

5 Polyvagal Theory – Stephen Porges

Dykema, Ravi
"Don't talk to me now, I'm scanning for danger"
How your nervous system sabotages your ability to relate
An interview with Stephen Porges about his polyvagal
theory. NEXUS March/April 2006

Porges, S.W. (1995). Orienting in a defensive world:
Mammalian modifications of our evolutionary
heritage. A Polyvagal Theory. Psychophysiology, 32,
301-318.

Porges, S.W. (1997). Emotion: An evolutionary by-
product of the neural regulation of the
autonomic nervous system. In C. S. Carter, B.
Kirkpatrick, & I.I. Lederhendler (eds.), The
Integrative Neurobiology of Affiliation, Annals of the
New York Academy of Sciences, 807, 62-77.

Porges, S.W. (1998). Love: An emergent property of the mammalian autonomic nervous system.
Psychoneuroendocrinology, 23, 837-861.

Porges, S.W. (2001). The Polyvagal Theory: Phylogenetic substrates of a social nervous system.
International Journal of Psychophysiology, 42, 123-146.

Porges, Stephen W. (2007),
The Polyvagal Perspective
Biol Psychol. 2007 February ; 74(2): 116–143.

Porges, Stephen W. (2009)
The polyvagal theory: New insights into adaptive reactions of the autonomic nervous system
CLEVELAND CLINIC JOURNAL OF MEDICINE
VOLUME 76 • SUPPLEMENT 2 APRIL 2009
doi:10.3949/ccjm.76.s2.17